Success Thru SERENITY

R.C. Pike

© Copyright 2008, R.C. Pike

All Rights Reserved.
No part of this book may be reproduced, stored in a
retrieval system, or transmitted by any means,
electronic, mechanical, photocopying, recording,
or otherwise, without written permission
from the author.

ISBN: 978-0-578-01638-2

This book is dedicated to everyone seeking the purpose and truth of life on earth and the way to find,
INNER PEACE, LOVE and SERENITY.

R.C. Pike

Success and serenity are not mutually exclusive concepts.

Success naturally flows in all areas of your life when you are serene. In serenity, your definition of success will change as well.

Achieve unlimited creativity, health, wellness and problem solving. No more human self imposed limits.

Serenity is tranquility, peace and contentment.

You make better decisions and perform better when you are at peace with yourself.

You have experienced other ways of dealing with life on earth, try serenity.

What has worrying and stress done for your life? They do not produce an effective way to live.

Humans often make their worst decisions when they are emotional and stressed.

On earth we experience confusion, worry and a full range of emotions.

You relate with others better when you are at peace.

Rise above the turbulence of human activity and let all pass below you unnoticed.

Looking at the earth from a distance, it looks like a calm, peaceful place. Try looking at your life from a distance as well.

Let go of the stress of human conditioning, judgments, opinions, prejudices, desires and emotions.

By gaining the perspective of calm detachment, you will avoid the actions and results of emotions.

We are able to give others great advice and love, do the same for yourself.

The world will always give you an emotional roller coaster ride any time you want it to. It is your choice to stay off the ride.

To reach serenity and maintain it, identify and release all that keeps you from inner peace.

Become a master of peace and tranquility. Go to the state of no concerns and stay there.

Do not let the ever-changing world affect you any more. Let it be.

When we keep ourselves detached and at peace, events that would normally bother us, occur without attention or concern.

Without attention there is no reaction.

With serenity, you avoid conflict with others. You no longer fuel the fire of confrontation.

Remain detached with no view, ego or position to defend.

Be in the world, but not of it.

Be open, light, energy.

Love and let live.

Detach from concerns. Let them go. Worrying doesn't help. It only makes you experience more of what you don't want to anyways.

Live in the solutions in life, not the problems. Live within.

Have you experienced enough of the human pinball machine?

Let go of who you think you are and be the real you.

You have no control over other's opinions, emotions, actions or judgments. Release them and be free.

Let go of identifying with your human personality. Identify with being what you really are.

Be open, quiet, calm and relaxed.

Do not take temporary earth experiences seriously.

Do not think so much. Our minds are torture chambers, always trying to figure out what they can't.

Feel your presence outside yourself. Be a bird, a river, a butterfly. Imagine being someone or something other than yourself.

The way to get rid of your worries is to stop paying attention to them and let them go.

Expectations, desires, judgments and attachments take away serenity. They are what keep you in the human pinball machine.

If you have no expectations, you will never be disappointed.

If you do not judge, you never need to forgive.

If you don't attach to people, pride or possessions, you won't feel the pain of disappointment, loss or rejection.

The sources of painful emotions are attachments, judgments, desires and expectations. Remove them and you remove suffering.

The only state that is real and permanent is serenity. All others are just temporary experiences.

Serenity is peace, truth, wisdom, creativity, understanding, love, contentment, fulfillment, joy and real success.

Desires open you to an emotional roller coaster that won't go away by fulfilling them, so why not just let them go?

Live simply. Release complications and stress.

Start experiencing a new life.

Think and speak sparingly.

Go with the flow.

Expect nothing from others. Let them experience what they want.

Be aware of the truth about this temporary life on earth.

We have always known there was something missing. With serenity, you are completely fulfilled.

Fear is worrying about what the future might bring. Serenity is the opposite of fear. When you are serene, you have no concerns about the future. You are fine, no matter what experiences pass your way.

The earth was the way it is before you came and will continue to be so after you leave. You have no control over it. You are not meant to. The earth has its purpose in the grand scheme of things. We are here for a brief moment to experience it.

We are energy temporarily experiencing humanity, not the other way around.

Enjoy without expectations or attachment. Let life flow.

Don't judge experiences as good or bad. You never know what is meant to happen anyways.

Picture a clear energy moving into different physical forms to experience the differences.

Be a quiet observer of life on earth.

It is not sad that life on earth is temporary. What is beyond this earth is so much more.

When you are serene, you are experiencing who you really are.

There is no interest in competing against others, or to try to be better than others. Simply enjoy your life with no concerns for what others say or do.

Meditation takes you to serenity.

Humans are often emotional. You don't need to be emotional with them. Allow others to feel what they are feeling without it affecting you.

By simplifying your life, you will find you have much more time and freedom.

Meditation is switching your awareness from the mind, concerns, emotions and desires to that of free flowing energy.

Meditate constantly to stay serene..Meditate throughout the day as you go about your functions.

Meditation is looking within instead of outside yourself to feel the way you want to.

Outside beauty constantly changes and eventually fades; inner beauty never changes or fades away.

When you stop seeking happiness from the world, bad habits, addictions and worries lose their power and disappear.

What happens in your life is irrelevant with serenity. Serenity does not come from good or bad events. Serenity comes only from within.

Humans spend a tremendous amount of time and energy worrying about that which they don't have any control over.

No matter who you are in this life, if you seek from the world, you will be taken on a roller coaster ride. That is the purpose of the earth. It does its job very well.

All through recorded history, the earth has taken its inhabitants on a highly emotional ride.

See you're self as a silent observer visiting earth from another realm to experience the differences.

If you believe you will feel serene if you have more of something from the world, try it and you find the opposite to be true. Very wealthy, famous and powerful people are often the most miserable. There is no amount of money, power or fame that will bring you lasting happiness or serenity.

If you believe you will be happy with the right person in your life, you will also be disappointed. Relationships quickly form into attachments, expectations and concerns.

Does this mean, you can't have nice things or relationships in your life and still have serenity? No, it simply means you can't look to things or relationships as your source of serenity. Find your unconditional, eternal source of love and serenity inside yourself and you will feel wonderful whether or not you have financial possessions or close relationships while on earth.

By not seeking from the outside and understanding the truth about this earth, you will be consistently serene, supportive and loving no matter what you face in life.

If you knew you lived eternally and were always safe, would you want to experience different worlds and realms?

If you were the creator of all life and love, would you allow your creations to experience what ever they wanted if they could not be harmed by the experiences?

The only thing you cannot give with a gift is the appreciation and understanding of that gift. That only comes with experience of the opposites.

As humans, we have a variety of personalities we experience. Sometimes we even wonder who it was that did something we did. We often here the expression, "I am sorry, I wasn't myself".

When you are experiencing thinking, emotions, worries or worldly desires, you are experiencing humanity. They do not exist in serenity.

Be an observer. Observe yourself. Completely let go and release your identity with this world and its ways.

Meditation is leaving the world of thinking and emotions and going to a state of peace, understanding and bliss.

Serenity is always there waiting for you. You will feel it with music, in nature, reading poetry or through spiritual words and meditation. Just let go of your worldly concerns and desires. Get away from your human identity and you will find serenity.

Meditation is the practice of quieting the turbulent mind and relaxing. As you practice being still and peaceful, you go deeper and deeper.

There is no anger, worry or bitterness in the state of serenity. All negative emotions disappear as you enter serenity.

We are not the temporary experience, we are the permanent experiencer.

You are not flesh, blood, bones, organs and water. That is what humans and other animals are comprised of on earth. You exist independently of the temporary human body. Fear, worry and suffering come from identifying with being human. Once you identify with your true nature, you will no longer suffer.

If you have ever seen a human body after death, you have seen that the life force is gone. What is gone is the real person. On earth, life and death is natural, like the seasons changing. Nothing is permanent on earth. That is the way it's meant to be.

Once you are at peace, what used to be important to you as a human will no longer matter. You will have no desire to control, manipulate or possess. The pressure of life is lifted. You go with the flow in full faith that you are safe and cannot be harmed. All negative judgments and emotions wash away.

In serenity, you no longer bounce from human mood to mood, reacting to others and life's events. You have escaped the human pinball machine.

Energy cannot be destroyed. You are energy.

If life on earth was a test, which should be tested, the all-knowing creator or the created, who has no idea what is going on?

If heavenly beings are at peace with complete knowledge of everything that is happening here on earth, why shouldn't we?

The creator is very aware of the different life forms on earth, including human's experience. Humans are born with strong instincts, emotions and desires. Humans do not control what they are born into. They just do the best they can to survive and succeed with what they have to work with.

If life on earth was a test with eternal consequences, heavenly beings would never be at peace waiting the outcomes of their loved ones on earth. What loving being would create animals on earth with strong instincts and desires and then punish them forever for what they did as a result of those desires and instincts? What loving creator creates anything to be punished?

There is no point in judging humans or any life on earth for doing what they instinctually do. The only philosophy or belief that makes any sense is that life on earth is an experience, not a test.

Life on earth is similar to the parable of the lost son in the bible.

We need to leave home to truly understand and appreciate what our home is.

Let go of the past. Let go of judgments and worries. You are loved. You are safe. You are eternally pure and perfect.

We know that the creator is love when we are serene. Love, joy and peace are all there is in serenity. It is the gift of universal life.

Completely letting go is extremely liberating.

What about our loved ones on earth? What about responsibilities, commitments, demands? Just smile and release them. Your loved ones are safe. You will be so much more loving, consistent and creative without fear and worry in your life. By letting go, you actually become more responsible and effective. You are no longer wasting time and energy trying to control what you can't anyways. Just love and let live with no expectations of others.

Fear and worry never help. They are natural emotions for humans, but do not exist in serenity. Living on earth with emotions that we do not experience in our natural state helps us to understand and appreciate how wonderful the gift of eternal life of serenity is.

When you are experiencing the part in, part-out state of serenity, you can easily be pulled in by worldly concerns, desires and attachments. To stay in serenity all the time requires a 100% release of all worldly desires, attachments and concerns. See them for the illusions they are. They have completed their mission of showing you the difference, allowing you to experience outside your natural realm.

Transcend the human influences. Ponder the truth. Meditate. Relax. Let go.

Go to serenity and stay there. Share with all from that peaceful, loving and creative state. There is no reason to let anything pull you back.

"Row, row, row your boat gently down the stream, merrily, merrily, merrily, merrily, life is but a dream".

We have everything we ever wanted. There is nothing outside that is of interest to us. There is nothing to chase after or desire. We are in the same peaceful, happy state with or without worldly possessions, relationships, praise or respect. Nothing can affect us any more, because we are finally aware of the truth about life on earth.

In serenity, your mind does not race like when you were experiencing being human. You are just aware, open, calm and peaceful.

In serenity your mind will relax. Human minds go through tremendous pressure trying to provide security and success.

The deeper you go in your meditations, the further you have to go back to experience the old life before meditation.

To find serenity is to simply return to your natural state outside earth.

Life on earth is always changing. Go with the flow. Don't judge or pay attention to the events in life. Just let them pass.

Realizing that you are not human is life changing. You will experience life on earth with awareness and peace.

By realizing life on earth is a temporary experience creating illusion; we can easily release our judgments, attachments and desires for worldly success, relationships and control.

We are all safe. There is nothing to worry about.

We do not need something else with serenity to feel wonderful.

Humans are so concerned about their reputations. Many even worry about how they will be remembered after they die.

Have no human identity to protect, defend or build up. You have no human identity period. There is nothing to hurt or offend.

Worldly desires and expectations keep you in the human pinball machine.

Once you have experienced the difference between serenity and desire based living, you will choose serenity. It's so much better.

Pay no attention to worldly matters.

In serenity, there are no competitions, judgments, controlling, power struggles, ego, jealousy or concerns.

Don't judge events in life as good or bad. You don't really know anyways. How many times have events that seemed bad led to something good and vice versa? Just let the world do its thing and let it be.

This earth is not fair. Innocent animals and people get hurt and killed every second. It is the nature of this realm of experience. It is how it was created to be.

Desires, attachments, fears and worries grow with attention and fade away with lack of attention.

Let others experience what they desire, just as you did. Don't interfere. It is all planned for the good of all. See the inner energy inside others. Be aware of the truth. Let go and relax.

What you are by creation is the only real lasting state of peace and happiness.

As you go through your days, practice oneness with the universal life force. Feel your energy being a part of everything.

Spend as much time as possible in silence. Simplify affairs. Eat simply and modestly. Let your body function without stress. Meditate and ponder truths constantly.

Meditation, consistency and perseverance open the door to a life of peace and joy.

Picture your self as light and energy capable of being anywhere and experiencing any thing.

You will experience that in which you put your attention and identification. Rise above. Be light and energy. Merge with the universal life force.

The greatest love and romance is with the universal spirit. It never grows old or boring. It never disappoints, judges or hurts.

There are no problems to solve or overcome.

The ultimate bliss is to let go of thinking, concerns and desires.

Realize the true nature of all human concerns, desires and emotions are empty and you will transcend the illusion of the earth.

There is nothing to save or change. We are all eternal, indestructible energy experiencing a different realm.

Meditation calms the mind. Eating right, simple exercise and yoga calms the body.

With serenity, you are free.

You are no longer who you thought you were.

Go with the flow wherever it takes you.

When you give, do so with no concern at all for a response.

Pay no attention to praise or criticism. Do not let others affect you in any way.

Are you still holding on to anything? Why?

When you are in serenity, you have the entire universe with you as a constant companion. You are never alone.

Relying on others for happiness is guaranteed to eventually disappoint.

All forms of temporary happiness on earth are just that, temporary. They will not last. They are not meant to.

Meditation is a personal practice.

Nothing can hurt or affect us on earth, so there is nothing to fear or worry about.

Humans are always chasing after something to feel better about themselves. They believe relationships, money, entertainment, sex, power, drugs, sports, education, fame, possessions, etc. are going to make them feel better. It is all an illusion. The irony is that all they have to do is stop chasing and relax and they will feel the way they want.

Fortunately, the human experience is a temporary one.

Practicing serenity takes us down a much more enjoyable path in life.

We have all had plenty of experiences with the opposite of serenity.

The only thing to pray for is serenity. With serenity all else comes naturally.

Many of us have spent most of our lives telling ourselves that we will be happy when this or that event occurs, when we reach our goal, meet the right person, get the job we are looking for, reach financial security, etc. The happiness does not last, so we seek a new goal, job, mate, etc. We were never just happy, peaceful and fulfilled without something else.

Relying on happiness from outside ourselves can never last because the world is always changing. It is made up of temporary experiences. It is not permanent, so it cannot bring permanent peace and happiness.

By choosing to live within, not outside ourselves, our lives simplify making serenity easier to obtain and maintain.

Stress, worrying, attachments and our egos just get in the way of creating success. We will have much more success with serenity than we ever would with our ego in charge. We are much more focused and creative when we are peaceful. When do you get the best ideas, in a state of stress or when you are relaxed? We all know this truth, but few practice it.

Completely let go of concern for what others think of you or want you to be.

Serenity makes everything better in our lives; improves our health, eliminates stress, simplifies finances, relationships, work, school and mental state.

Serenity is an inside/out approach. The world is generally outside/in.

When you tune out the outside material world, what is left? What's left is the truth.

When you are in the light of serenity, you don't care about all that is happening on earth.

Everything you are seeking has always been with you.

Be outwardly accommodating and inwardly clear, open and serene. What others say or do to you is irrelevant.

Welcome change as a part of life.

True power, joy and creativity are in freedom, not control. You cannot control other people for long.

When you have calmed your emotions with the truth about expectations and attachments; random passing thoughts just pass on. With time and practice, even passing thoughts stop coming.

You can't be in two realms at once. Where your attention is, you are.

Remember when you were a child it was still you inside.

Imagine being someone else or something else. Is it still you inside observing? You can experience different things, but it is always you as the observer.

You will easily get through all trials in life by realizing it is just a passing experience that cannot harm you in any way.

Stay aware. Stay calm.

Do not pay attention to other's temporary experiences.

Stay mentally quiet and unconcerned.

Keep your mind inactive, clean, clear and open.

Leave the realm of worldly concerns. No concern for past, future or present.

Reunite with the universal life force and be fulfilled.

Do not burden yourself with views, opinions or judgments.

No longer see yourself as an individual. You are a part of everything.

See your true nature and be that.

Use openness and emptiness to receive the universe.

Realize there is no human self. Today it is here tomorrow it is gone. It is just a passing experience that is not real.

Detach from everything worldly. Be energy.

Start your days with meditation and detachment. Do not let worldly concerns enter into your awareness.

There is a peace and harmony beyond the turmoil of this earth.

You are not your body. You are not your mind. You are not your personality. You are not your past. You are not your emotions.

Avoid the constant company of other people. Enjoy time alone to relax and meditate.

Don't let any thing or any one affect your serenity.

Your joy from meditation will be greater than anything you have experienced from the material world.

Do things calmly. Be content.

Let things be and you will be serene. Trying to change or control things causes stress.

Once you rediscover your true nature, you will be continuously happy.

Our natural state is eternal. Our human state is temporary.

There is no end to human desires. Let them go.

When you let go, you let go of everything you don't want. What is left is peace and happiness. You will feel a sense of oneness, fulfillment and wonder.

Accept life as life and nothing ever goes wrong.

Your relationships will improve when you let go of expectations and judgments of others. You will be consistently loving and supportive of the people in your life.

By continually pondering serene thoughts and images, you transcend into serenity.

You are timeless and universal.

Human lives go along with circumstances. Spiritual lives stay secure and peaceful.

Stay aware of the truth of who you really are.

Are you human that transforms to energy when you die? No, you have to be energy all along.

By changing your identity from being a human body to being energy inside a human body, you will naturally take care of the body. The desires to over eat or in any way abuse the body will leave.

Changing thinking and habits are difficult at first, but become much easier and natural with time and consistency.

Do not waste any energy on negative thoughts, worries or concerns.

Energy is real and lasting. Human events and circumstances are just passing experiences.

The earth is an interesting place to visit, but you wouldn't want to live here forever.

There is no permanence on earth. Change is the normal state.

Don't rely on the human mind any more. It does not understand what is really going on. Do not pay attention to passing thoughts.

One of the last experiences on earth is to experience the earth with awareness and serenity.

There is nothing real to hold on to on earth. Release your burdens and concerns for good.

By transcending thoughts, you become clear and open.

Let go of desires to possess, control or have your way.

When you are at peace, the right ideas naturally flow to you.

A great deal of human stress and misery comes from our egos.

Serenity is secure and dynamic at the same time.

Serenity comes from being the real you.

Turn your home into a sanctuary.

Leave the fear based world behind.

Success and happiness are in the process, not the end results.

Seeking rewards only, leads to the ends justifying the means philosophy.

Spiritual masters remove themselves from the contradictions of human concerns, desires, expectations and attachments.

There is no depression, anxiety, fear, worry, or anger in serenity. They cannot coexist. They are completely different wavelengths.

Look past temporary experiences. We are on this earth for a blink in time.

No outside person or event has any impact on your serenity unless you let it. There are no valid reasons to let them.

By eliminating negative emotional states, you eliminate negative actions and consequences.

Focus on the inside and the outside will take care of itself.

Universal Spirit is serenity. That is our true nature.

There is no stability on earth. It is always changing, dealing with wars, disasters, rumors, scandals, diseases, accidents and death.

The more you seek happiness and peace from outside yourself, the more out of balance you will feel.

Knowing your self is freedom. All burdens and misconceptions are lifted.

Universal energy loves you. It is love. You will feel it. It never disappoints. It is the greatest joy there is. Trust it.

This world shows us that we do not need anything else for complete fulfillment, peace and joy. The spiritual energy we are created in contains everything.

What you have experienced in the past is not you. You are not a human experience. Let the past go.

Go from thinking, worrying and feeling emotional to having serenity flow through you.

Feel the pressure leave. No more ego or reputation to defend. There is nothing to worry about. You know the truth.

Just trying to change the human self keeps you on the roller coaster. Transcend the human self. No longer identify with a temporary body. Identify with the eternal energy inside you that existed before your body and continues on after it doesn't.

Stay detached and aware.

Knowing the truth is awareness. Living the truth is enlightment.

The real you is energy, not flesh and bones. You are invisible, open and clear. You are capable of going anywhere and experiencing anything.

When situations occur in life, stay aloof and act upon inner promptings.

The real you cannot be hurt. You do not fear anything. You cannot be offended. You are peace and love.

You will notice a huge difference in how you feel and how your days go when you meditate before starting any activities in the morning.

Have no mind, no concerns, no ego, no desires and you will find peace.

You have to lose your self to find yourself. Lose your human self to find your true self.

Living in serenity is not only the best way to live eternally; it is the best way to live on earth.

Do not attach to people or possessions. Be the same with or without anyone or anything.

The answer has been with you all along as you have chased in the world looking for it.

Turn your attention inward, not outward.

Do not mind other people's business.

Be cooperative and accommodating. Give when asked with no interest in return or gratitude.

The earth is doing its job. Everyone is safe.

If you can't believe in the creator of everything, what can you believe in?

You feel the truth when you quiet the mind, relax and meditate.

Instead of trying to feel serenity occasionally or just in times of trouble, let serenity be your constant companion.

Have no concerns for the future. With serenity guiding you, you will go through all situations as if they don't exist.

The Creator of all loves you. What is there to fear?

Always remember, this earth is a realm of temporary, material experiences. You are from a different realm. This is temporary. You are permanent.

You can finally relax. There is nothing to worry about. We are all safe.

By simplifying your life and affairs, worldly pressures and concerns will diminish and fade away.

When you live in serenity, you will never be prompted to do anything harmful. You will not have bad thoughts. Eventually, even your dreams will be peaceful.

With serenity, you do not waste any energy. This allows you to be much more effective and focused when you are accomplishing a task.

Others may take advantage of you at times, but you won't care. You always have the choice to remove your self from unwanted or unhealthy environments.

In your relationships, you will always be calm and stable. You are aware of what others are going through and you don't take it personally. You have no demands, expectations or reactions with others.

Simplify your diet. Eat wholesome, natural foods and serenity will be easier to reach and maintain.

If you are overweight or addicted to a substance, you will be lifted from your addictions when you live in serenity. You will be detached from your body and treat it with care. Your mind and body will no longer control your actions the way they have in the past.

Do not judge yourself, others or events. No processing of good or bad. Simply let things be as they are.

You have no control over the events on this earth. You are not meant to be. You are not here to change things. You are here to experience.

If anyone is mean to you, respond with awareness and kindness. If anyone is nice to you and praises you, respond with awareness and kindness.

Life is not a contest. You have nothing to prove.

Enjoy the opportunity to experience life in a different realm. There is plenty to experience on earth.

If you have no expectations or judgments of others, you will have no reactions to their words or actions.

Go deeper and deeper into your meditations and serenity.

With serenity, there is nothing to escape from. You feel wonderful just being you.

Disconnect from earthly attention. Let go of the past. Let go of labels.

We all leave the earth the way we came, perfect, pure energy.

You cannot hurt energy.

Keep the mind turned off and have a wonderful day.

Peaceful living is not only the most joyous way to live; it is the most effective and practical way as well. You are so much more creative and effective operating with out fear in your life.

"We must not cease from exploration and the end of all our exploring will be to arrive where all began and know the place for the first time."

-T.S. Elliot

Life on earth including humanity is an extremely limited form of existence.

We will all have experienced life from its different perspectives. We will all have felt the full range of human emotions. That is the whole purpose of why the earth exists.

Do not seek to be liked, understood or appreciated.

Do not even wish for certain experiences, other than serenity, to occur for yourself or others. Let life flow as it is supposed to.

Most humans are very reactionary. Their moods are completely subject to the words or action of others around them. They do not take ownership of their feelings or actions. They let the world do it for them.

The earthly illusion is very convincing until you relax and meditate, and then the truth shines through.

Let go of everything all the time.

Have no identity or intellect to defend.

Desires, concerns and problems never go away if you deal with them from the human perspective. They are not meant to. Eliminate them by transcending them, not constantly giving them attention.

Do not let the outside in.

Every day life is full of examples of why the serenity realm is so different and wonderful compared to life on earth. Thank the creator for loving us so much that we share in the ultimate joy of universal love and serenity for all eternity.

Don't get mixed up with worldly matters.

Love with no expectations or attachments.

Thoughts, desires, ego, concerns and worries just mask the real you.

There is no way to satisfy a fearful mind through worldly activities.

Think ahead 150 years. Every human and animal now living will be replaced by new beings trying to survive and succeed in a fear based, competitive world. The players will change. The experience will be the same.

Feel the continual calm waves of peace and joy flowing through you.

With the universe life force with you, you can do or be anything.

Relationships change dramatically. You no longer look to take from relationships. You are no longer possessive or controlling. You are free to truly love unconditionally.

Imagine your human body has died. Leave your body and rise above. See your human body left behind. Look at all the other humans. You are still you. You just no longer have any fear or concerns.

Identify with being universal energy, not being a human and you are free. Be free. Fly around. Say goodbye to the human self. Experience a completely new life free from all that dragged you down in the past.

Release the human identity. There is no one to impress. Set it free into the world of illusion where it belongs.

When you reach the point where nothing bothers you, you are free and you will experience amazing success.

If you are experiencing suffering in your life, you are tuning in to the human channel. There is no suffering in the serenity channel. To end your suffering, switch channels.

You are unconditionally loved by the source of all life.

In serenity, there is no better or worse. We all experience the same universal energy flowing through us. There is no desire to be better than others. We are from the same source experiencing in our own unique ways.

In most ways the earth shows us the opposite of what we continually experience with serenity.

With serenity, you receive all you are looking for in your life plus much more that you even knew existed.

On earth, we experience being alone and isolated. By connecting with the universal life force through serenity, you are no longer alone. You are no longer an individual facing all of life's challenges. You are a part of the universal energy that creates everything.

Desires, attachments, expectations and concerns keep you in the human realm. Let them all go and you will experience the joy and truth of who you really are.

Life on earth is very competitive and often stressful. In the animal kingdom, the strong survive and reproduce. More From childhood, humans are judged, graded and labeled.

Humans are judged more for the color of their skin, height, weight, families, education, appearances, possessions, intelligence, strength, talent, accomplishments, past, money, clothes, friends, etc., etc.

With all the constant judging, it is no wonder humans have strong desires to have worldly accomplishments, possessions, education and beauty. We are taught that the rich and beautiful have the best lives. We try to impress others with our possessions and accomplishments. These desires keep humans on the emotional roller coaster.

You will be amazed at how wonderful life becomes again by letting go of all the human desires and conditioning and going back to just being you with no concern about the world.

Serenity always awaits us when we are ready to tune out the world and tune in universal energy.

Life on earth is not fair. It is not meant to be.

Your body and life on earth function better with serenity. Stress, fear, anger and worry are not conducive to healthy living.

There is no better place to be than serenity. Life on earth proves that.

We learn the difference by experiencing opposites.

You are serene no matter what is happening on earth when you know the truth about what is really going on.

The promise of fame and fortune are an illusion. No matter what you are experiencing, you are still you. You can't escape yourself.

With Serenity there is no burden to carry. You let go of all worldly concerns and live free.

www.ingramcontent.com/pod-product-compliance
Lightning Source LLC
Chambersburg PA
CBHW040911020526
44116CB00026B/28